822.91SHA

THIS BOOK SHOULD BE RETURNED ON OR BEFORE THE LATEST
DATE SHOWN TO THE LIBRARY _____ IT WAS BORROWED

LOAN FROM Z

24 FEB 1993

LOAN FROM Z

15. 21 DEC 1993
JUN 94

08. JUL 94

D0571404

**AUTHOR**

Shaffer, P

**CLASS**

822.91SHA

**TITLE**

The Public Eye

Lancashire
County
Council

THE LANCASHIRE LIBRARY.
Library Headquarters,
143, Corporation St.,
PRESTON PRI 2TB.

a30118 047876291b

1.50

© 1962 BY PETER SHAFFER LTD

*This play is fully protected under the copyright laws of the British Commonwealth of Nations, the United States of America, and all countries of the Berne and Universal Copyright Conventions.*

*All rights are strictly reserved.*

*It is an infringement of the copyright to give any public performance or reading of this play either in its entirety or in the form of excerpts without the prior consent of the copyright owners. No part of this publication may be transmitted, stored in a retrieval system, or reproduced in any form or by any means, electronic, mechanical, photocopying, manuscript, typescript, recording, or otherwise, without the prior permission of the copyright owners.*

Please note our NEW ADDRESS:

Samuel French Ltd
52 Fitzroy Street London W1P 6JR
Tel: 01 - 387 9373

..., STRAND, LONDON WC2E 7JE, or their authorized agents, issue licences to amateurs to give performances of this play on payment of a fee. The fee must be paid and the licence obtained before a performance is given.

Licences are issued subject to the understanding that it shall be made clear in all advertising that the audience will witness an amateur performance; and that the names of the authors of the plays shall be included on all announcements and on all programmes.

The royalty fee indicated below is subject to contract and subject to variation at the sole discretion of Samuel French Ltd.

Basic fee for each and every
performance by amateurs          Code F
in the British Isles

In theatres or halls seating 600 or more the fee will be subject to negotiation.

In territories overseas the fee quoted above may not apply. Application must be made to our local authorized agents, or if there is no such agent, to Samuel French Ltd, London.

Applications to perform the play by professionals should be made to CHRISTOPHER MANN LTD, 140 Park Lane, London W1.

ISBN 0 573 02219 4

MADE AND PRINTED IN GREAT BRITAIN BY
LATIMER TREND AND CO. LTD, PLYMOUTH
MADE IN ENGLAND

# THE PUBLIC EYE

Produced together with *The Private Ear* by H. M. Tennent Ltd at the Globe Theatre, London, on the 10th May 1962, with the following cast of characters:

*(in the order of their appearance)*

| | |
|---|---|
| JULIAN CRISTOFOROU | *Kenneth Williams* |
| CHARLES SIDLEY, a chartered accountant | *Richard Pearson* |
| BELINDA SIDLEY, his wife | *Maggie Smith* |

Directed by PETER WOOD

Décor by RICHARD NEGRI

*The action of the Play passes in Charles Sidley's offices in Bloomsbury, on a summer morning*

*Time—the present*

# THE PUBLIC EYE

SCENE—*The outer office of Charles Sidley, Chartered Accountant, in Bloomsbury. A summer morning.*

*It is a lofty room with two tall, sash windows* R, *overlooking the street. A door* LC *leads into the hall of the building and when this door is open we can see stairs going up to higher floors. A door* RC *leads into Charles' inner office and is marked* "PRIVATE". *The remainder of the back wall consists of tall bookshelves laden with works of reference. There is a desk* C, *where a secretary customarily sits, a settee under the windows and a combined chair and set of library steps* L. *In the corner up* RC *there is a large Cloisonne vase used as an umbrella-stand. There is a swivel chair behind the desk. There are Bokhara rugs in front of each door and in front of the desk. A pair of Chinese statuettes stand on the window-sills. On the desk there is an external telephone; an intercom and a press-button arrangement for admitting callers. The desk has drawers both back and front. There are light switches* L *of the door* LC. *The inner office has two windows at the back overlooking the street and is furnished with a desk, two chairs and a rug. On the desk there is the usual dressing, a telephone, and a brass table-lamp. The intercom system has a microphone and speaker off* L. *The offstage microphone is controlled with a switch. Belinda's voice, in due course, is heard through the speaker on the desk. The dialogue is worked* "live".

*The room should present an air of stylization achieved through the use of very few colours: walls and woodwork pure white; the books russet and gold. The furniture must be excellent. Avoid clutter and inelegance.*

*When the* CURTAIN *rises, it is mid-morning on a Saturday. Bright sunlight streams through the windows* R. CHARLES' *umbrella is in the stand up* R, *with his bowler hat on the handle. The doors are closed. Standing* C, *with his back to the audience looking at his wrist watch, is* JULIAN CHRISTOFOROU. *He is a man in his middle thirties; his whole air breathes a gentle eccentricity, a nervousness combined with an air of almost meek self-disapprobation and a certain bright detachment. His speech in the main is rapid and virtuostic in effect. As the play proceeds he must be seen and heard to grow in authority, from a deceptively ineffective figure in a comic magus. At the moment he is bundled in a white raincoat. His brief-case, a capacious leather affair in the manner of a Gladstone-bag, is on the floor c. After a moment he picks it up and wanders L. He studies the book-shelves, puts his case on the floor and moves the chair/steps to see the lower shelves. He then leans on the chair and to his surprise, it tips. He examines the chair and discovers it tips right over to form the library steps. He climbs the steps and sits on the top of them, facing R. He takes a large yellow silk handkerchief from one pocket and spreads it over his knees. From another pocket he produces a packet of raisins and pours them out on to the handkerchief. He just begins to eat them when he cocks his ear, hastily stuffs the handkerchief and its contents into another pocket and sits upright and unconcerned as* CHARLES SIDLEY *enters* RC, *from the inner office.* CHARLES *is a man of forty, with a fairly steady line in pompous sarcasm, and another, more immediately concealed, in self-pity. He is humming "The Bolero" and does not notice Julian. He pauses in the doorway, takes out his keys, closes and locks the door, then picks up his bowler hat, puts it on and takes his umbrella from the stand. He goes to the upstage window* R *and fastens it. As he does so,* JULIAN *comes quietly down the steps and crosses up behind Charles.* CHARLES *goes to the downstage window and fastens it.* JULIAN *follows.* CHARLES, *still not seeing Julian, crosses below the desk to the door* LC. JULIAN *remains behind the settee, and speaks as Charles reaches the door.*

JULIAN. Good morning.

(CHARLES *reacts violently with surprise and turns*)

CHARLES. Good morning.
JULIAN. Mr Sidley?
CHARLES. Correct.
JULIAN. I'm delighted.
CHARLES. You want to see me?

JULIAN. It's rather more than I have to. (*He moves in front of the settee*) Not that I don't want to see you, of course.

CHARLES. Well, I'm sorry, but I was just on my way home. The office isn't really open on Saturday mornings. I was just doing a little work.

JULIAN. I know. I saw you.

CHARLES (*removing his bowler*) I beg your pardon?

JULIAN. I peeped into your office before. But you were so engaged I didn't like to disturb you.

CHARLES (*moving to L of the desk*) How long have you been waiting, then.

JULIAN. About half an hour.

CHARLES. Half . . .

JULIAN. Oh, please don't apologize. It's a positive joy to wait in a room like this. There are so many delights to detain one. Your reference books, for instance. Overwhelming!

CHARLES. Thank you. (*He moves behind the desk*)

JULIAN. I perceive you have a passion for accuracy. (*He crosses below the desk to L*)

CHARLES. Let's say, a respect for fact. (*He puts his umbrella in the stand and hangs his bowler on the handle*)

JULIAN. Oh, let's indeed. I do admire that. Mind you, one must be careful. Facts can become an obsession. I hope they aren't with you.

CHARLES. I hope so, too. (*He moves behind the desk*) Now, if you don't mind—perhaps I can make an appointment for next week.

JULIAN (*ignoring Charles and staring at the shelves*) Websters! Chambers! Whitakers Almanac! Even the names have a certain leathery beauty. And how imposing they look on shelves. Serried ranks of learning.

CHARLES. Are you a salesman?

JULIAN. Forgive me. I was lapsing. Yes, I was once. But then I was everything once. I had twenty-three positions before I was thirty.

CHARLES. Did you really?

JULIAN (*facing Charles*) I know what you're thinking. A striking record of failure. But you're wrong. I never fail in jobs, they fail me. The life goes out of them. Selling reference books looked very hopeful to begin with. Offering Treasuries of Knowledge to homes that otherwise had only the Television Quiz as a source of information seemed useful and kind. (*He moves to* L *of the desk*) The last man I sold a *Brittanica* to was a self-made Glaswegian who was obviously just going to use it to crush his teen-age son on dull points of reference. When I sent him the bill, I enclosed a note reading: "Brilliance does not lie in knowing endless rows of facts, but in mobility of mind." He complained to my boss, and I was fired. Forgive me, I'm talking too much.

CHARLES. That's perfectly all right. All the same, I really must be getting home now. I'm sorry to have kept you waiting, even inadvertently. (*He puts on his spectacles*) May I make an appointment for you early next week?

JULIAN. Certainly. If that's what you want.

CHARLES. Well, as I say, I don't receive clients at the week-end. (*He sits at the desk*) Now, let me look at my secretary's book. (*He refers to an appointments book*) What about next Tuesday?

JULIAN (*considering*) I don't really like Tuesdays. (*He crosses below the desk to* RC) They're an indeterminate sort of day.

CHARLES (*with a touch of exasperation*) Well, you name it, Mr . . . ?

JULIAN. "Cristoforou."

CHARLES. Cristoforou?

JULIAN. Yes. It's a little downbeat, I admit. Balkan cigarettes and conspirator moustaches. I don't care for it, but it's not to be avoided. (*He moves to* R *of the desk*) My father was a Rhodes Scholar. I mean he was a scholar from Rhodes.

CHARLES (*with desperate politeness*) Oh, yes?

JULIAN. Why don't you call me "Julian"? That's a good between-the-wars name. Cricket pads and a secret passion for Virginia Woolf. That's my mother's influence. She had connexions with Bloomsbury. A boarding-house, to be precise.

CHARLES. Would you please tell me when you would like to see me?

JULIAN. It's rather more when *you* would like, isn't it?

CHARLES. I have no special relationship with the days of the week, Mr Cristoforou.

JULIAN. Oh, no more have I, in the final analysis. I mean, they don't actually prevent me from doing things on them. They merely encourage or discourage.

CHARLES. Well, shall we say Tuesday, then?

JULIAN. Yes. If that's the soonest you can manage it.

CHARLES. I suppose I could squeeze you in late on Monday if it's urgent.

JULIAN. I had imagined it was. In fact, I must admit to feeling quite disappointed. (*He crosses to the steps* L)

CHARLES. I'm sorry . . .

JULIAN. No, if the truth be known, extremely surprised. (*He picks up his brief-case*)

CHARLES. Surprised?

JULIAN. At your being so offhand. I had imagined you differently.

CHARLES. Are you in some kind of trouble?

JULIAN. Your trouble is mine, sir. It's one of my mottoes. Not inappropriate, I think. Still, of course, I mustn't be unreasonable. It's your decision. After all, you're paying. (*He moves to the door* LC)

CHARLES. I'm what?

JULIAN (*opening the door*) Paying.

CHARLES (*rising*) Mr Cristoforou, come here. (*He moves to* L *of the desk*) We seem to be talking at cross purposes.

JULIAN (*closing the door and moving to* L *of Charles*) Oh, not cross, I hope. I hate scenes.

CHARLES. I had assumed you were here to see me professionally.

JULIAN. Certainly.

CHARLES. Well?

JULIAN. Well, it's more you wishing to see me, isn't it? Or hear from me, anyway.

CHARLES. Perhaps you'd better state your business with me very precisely.

JULIAN. You mean to say you don't know it?

CHARLES. How can I?

JULIAN. You don't know why I'm here?

CHARLES. I haven't the faintest idea.

JULIAN (*crossing below Charles to* c) How appalling! I'm agonized. I'm really agonized. What must you think of me? Chattering away and you not even knowing why I'm here. Well, of course, I'd assumed—but then you shouldn't assume anything. Certainly not in my business. I'm afraid it's absolutely typical of me. My wits are scattered when they should be most collected. (*He puts his brief-case on the desk and opens it*) You haven't got a spoon, by any chance?

CHARLES. A spoon?

JULIAN. For my Yoghurt. Forgive me, it's a distressing symptom of nervousness which I've never been able to conquer. I always eat when I'm embarrassed. Or, as in this case, agonized. (*He takes a carton of Yoghurt from his brief-case, removes the lid, licks the lid and puts it in the brief-case*)

CHARLES. Mr Cristoforou, I'm not noted for my patient disposition.

JULIAN. I'm glad to hear that. Patience too long controlled turns to cruelty. Old Persian proverb. At least, I think it's Persian. It could be Hindu. (*He crosses to the book-case* L) Do you have a Dictionary of Proverbs?

CHARLES (*bluntly*) Who are you?

JULIAN. I'm Parkinson's replacement.

CHARLES. Replacement?

JULIAN (*moving to* L *of Charles*) From Mayhew and Figgis. (*He takes out a visiting card and gives it to Charles*) Now, there are two names which are quite inappropriate for a detective agency. They should be bootmakers to the Duke of Cumberland, or something like that. Don't you agree? (*He crosses and picks up his brief-case*)

CHARLES. Are you telling me that you are an official employee of Mayhew and Figgis?

JULIAN (*crossing to the library steps*) Of course. What else? (*He puts his brief-case on the steps and takes out a sugar canister*) I'm here to make our monthly report. The office was to telephone you and say I'd be coming today. (*The canister is apparently empty and he returns it to the brief-case*) They obviously failed. Very embarrassing. For both of us. Very.

CHARLES. And you are here in place of Parkinson?

JULIAN. Exactly.

CHARLES. Why? Where is he?

JULIAN. He's not with us any more

CHARLES. You mean he resigned?

JULIAN. No. He was thrown down a lift shaft in Goodge Street. Do you know it? It's off the Tottenham Court Road . . .

CHARLES (*irritated*) I know where it is.

JULIAN. Hazards of the game, you know. No-one mourns him more than I. (*He crosses above Charles to the up* R *corner of the desk, gives Charles a bright smile, opens a drawer in the desk and extracts a spoon*) Where there's a secretary, there's always a teaspoon.

(CHARLES *stares at Julian in disbelief, then impulsively lifts the telephone receiver*)

What are you doing?

(CHARLES *dials grimly*)

CHARLES (*into the telephone*) Hallo? . . . Mayhew and Figgis? . . . This is Mr Sidley. Mr Charles Sidley. I'd like to speak to Mr Mayhew. If he's not there I should like his home number . . . Yes . . . Good. Thank you . . .

(JULIAN *moves to the upstage window* R *and eats his Yoghurt*)

(*He sits at the desk. Irritably*) Hallo? . . . Mr Mayhew? . . . Mr Sidley here . . . I have a man in my office at this moment calling himself . . .

JULIAN (*meekly*) Cristoforou.

CHARLES (*into the telephone*) Cristoforou. He claims to be an employee of yours . . . What? . . . Yes? . . . Oh . . . Oh, I see . . . Yes, he told me that. Goodge Street . . . (*Exasperated*) I know where it is . . . Very regrettable. A most efficient man . . . (*He looks at Julian*) He is? . . . Well, I hope I can, Mr Mayhew, I hope I can. This is a very delicate matter, as you know . . . What? . . . No, of course I understand that; yours is a firm of the very highest . . . Yes, I say I know; yours is a firm of the very highest . . . Yes, yes, of course: I realize that . . . Naturally. Yours is a firm of the very highest . . . Well, we'll see, Mr Mayhew. I am always willing to give people the benefit of the doubt, though I may add that when I say doubt in this case, I mean doubt. Good morning. (*He replaces the receiver*) You have a garrulous employer. (*He removes his spectacles and puts them in his pocket*)

JULIAN (*moving to R of the desk and putting the empty carton and spoon on it*) Only where he feels his honour to be at stake. After all, his is a firm of the very highest . . . (*He smiles his bright smile*)

(CHARLES *glares*)

In this case he said I'd been with it for three years and did the most expert work. Yes?

CHARLES. Correct, as it happens.

JULIAN. Well, it happens to be true. At the risk of sounding forward, I am a superb detective. It's one of the few jobs where being nondescript is an advantage. (*He moves to the settee*)

CHARLES. One would hardly describe you as nondescript, Mr Cristoforou.

JULIAN. Oh, yes. I attained nondescript a long time ago. Last year I became characterless. This year, superfluous. Next year I shall be invisible. It's rather like one of those American Gain Confidence Courses in reverse. Make Nothing of Yourself in Six Easy Lessons. Actually, I've been working on your affair for four weeks. Mayhew's is a large agency, and we often take over each other's assignments. It's quite routine.

CHARLES. All the same, a little high-handed, I'd say.

JULIAN. I'm sorry you'd say that.

CHARLES. In any case, how did you know I was here?

JULIAN. I am a detective, Mr Sidley. You work here every Saturday morning and your wife goes to the *Cordon Bleu* for a cooking lesson.

CHARLES. Correct.

JULIAN. It was an obvious opportunity to come round.

CHARLES. I see. Very thorough, I'm sure. (*He rises and moves to R of the desk*) Now, perhaps you would oblige me by reading your report.

JULIAN (*crossing to his brief-case*) Of course. That's why I'm here.

CHARLES. One would never know it.

(JULIAN *gropes in the brief-case. He struggles with it for a moment and produces not the report but an immense plastic bag of macaroons*)

JULIAN. Macaroons—would you like one? (*He moves to* L *of the desk*) Excuse me. It's really disgusting, this eating business, I know. I have a friend who's a barrister, and he gets so nervous about speaking in court, he eats sweets all day long. In his last murder case he devoured twenty-six fudge bars in a morning. You're not a lawyer, are you? (*He puts the macaroons on the desk*)

CHARLES. No.

JULIAN (*moving to the library steps*) Of course not: an accountant. (*He takes a greasy foolscap folder from his brief-case, puts the brief-case on the floor, then sits on the top of the steps*) Silly of me. Scattered wits again. That's almost like being a priest today, isn't it? I mean, people do what you tell them without question. What did Parkinson tell you at your last meeting?

CHARLES. Surely you know that already, if you inherited his assignment.

JULIAN. His report was negative.

CHARLES. Correct.

JULIAN. Your suspicions were unfounded.

CHARLES. So he said. The point is, are they still? A month has gone by since then.

JULIAN. That rather depends on what they were, doesn't it?

CHARLES. You know very well what they were. What they always are when you call in a detective. Are you trying to be humorous?

JULIAN. I sometimes succeed in being humorous, Mr Sidley, but I never try. Suspicion is a highly subjective word. It refers with exactitude only to the man who entertains it.

CHARLES (*moving to* L *of the desk*) Mr Cristoforou: what do I have to do to get from you the information I am paying for?

JULIAN (*reasonably*) I don't know what that is, Mr Sidley. If you wish to know whether your wife is being sexually

unfaithful to you, I must point out that it is extremely
hard for a private eye to witness copulation.

CHARLES. How dare you?

JULIAN. It's even more difficult to witness the *desire* for
copulation. Inevitably, therefore, there is no proof that
your wife has slept outside her marriage bed.

CHARLES. No proof.

JULIAN. None whatever.

CHARLES. Then you have nothing to tell me.

JULIAN. I wouldn't say that.

CHARLES. Then what would you say? In a word, what
—would—you—say?

JULIAN. I haven't got a word.

CHARLES. Then find one!

JULIAN (*hastily*) Perhaps I'd better read my report. (*He
tries to open the folder but unfortunately the pages seem to be
gummed together*) Oh, dear. That's treacle.

CHARLES. What?

JULIAN. I tried to transport a waffle yesterday, but it
didn't work. (*He tries for a long moment to separate the pages of
his report. It tears badly*) Oh, dear! I'm agonized, I am
really. How can you ever forgive me enough? I mean,
how can I ever be forgiven enough? No, that's not what I
mean. (*He looks at Charles with hapless eyes*)

(CHARLES *stares at Julian in a thunderous silence*)

(*Ingratiatingly*) Well, I can read the first page, anyway. (*He
refers to the first page, which is in two pieces and reads in an official
voice*) "Report by J. Cristoforou on the movements of
Mrs Charles Sidley. Wednesday, September the twenty-
second." That was my first day, you see.

CHARLES (*crossing above the desk to* R) Never mind about
that.

JULIAN (*reading*) "Ten-forty-eight subject leaves house
Takes taxi at corner of Walton and Pont Street." That's
always a tricky one, by the way. Have you ever considered
what one does if one's quarry hails a taxi and there isn't
another in sight?

CHARLES. I'd always assumed you drove a car.

JULIAN. Oh, no, not in London. The parking is too

difficult, and the police make no allowance for us amateurs.

CHARLES. Continue, please.

JULIAN (*reading*) "Subject proceeds to Madame Martha, hatmaker, of thirty-two Marble Street."

CHARLES. Could you see in?

JULIAN. Yes.

CHARLES. Who was there?

JULIAN. Four other ladies.

CHARLES. Any men?

JULIAN. I don't think so.

CHARLES. You don't think . . . ?

JULIAN. I mean they may have been dressed as ladies. It's just a possibility in a hatshop.

CHARLES. I see.

JULIAN (*reading*) "Subject collects hat, which appears to be already ordered, and emerges wearing it. Hat resembles bunch of stinging nettles. Very unbecoming."

CHARLES. Watch what you say, please. Everything my wife knows about hats, or clothes of any kind, she learnt from me. When I first met her she wore nothing but sweaters and trousers. When you criticize her taste in hats, you are criticizing me.

JULIAN. I'm terribly sorry. (*He rises, comes from the steps and moves above the desk*)

CHARLES. I suppose it's only natural that now she's moved away from me she should revert to type. All this last week she's worn nothing but a hideous black sombrero.

JULIAN. You don't like it?

CHARLES. You do?

JULIAN. I think it has a certain gamin chic.

CHARLES (*facing front*) Continue, please.

JULIAN (*reading*) "Eleven-thirty subject in—(*he moves close to Charles and speaks into his left ear*) exquisite green hat—(*he crosses behind Charles to* R) walks up Brompton Road, enters *The Hanging Gardens Coffee Bar*. (*He moves behind the settee, then down* R) Orders a Babylon Special."

CHARLES. What the hell's that?

JULIAN. A confection of peppermint ice-cream, chocolate chips and molasses. Your wife is rather partial to it. So am I, as a matter of irrelevant fact. Do you like ice-cream?

CHARLES. I'm afraid not. What happened next?

JULIAN (*reading*) "Twelve-seventeen subject rises and walks to Kensington Gardens. Walked to the statue called Physical Energy." That's a man controlling a horse.

CHARLES. I know what it is. What did she do?

JULIAN. She looked at it and laughed. A curious reaction, I thought.

CHARLES. Not at all. The first week we were married I showed her that statue and explained to her precisely why it was ridiculous. When you criticize her taste in statuary you criticize me.

JULIAN. I don't know where to look.

CHARLES. At your report.

JULIAN. Yes. Certainly.

CHARLES. She was waiting for someone, I presume.

JULIAN. On the contrary, she wandered about quite aimlessly.

CHARLES. How do you know it was aimlessly?

JULIAN. At one point she picked up some acorns.

CHARLES. Acorns?

JULIAN. Yes: to throw at the ducks. I got the impression she had nothing better to do.

CHARLES. Charming! That's the rest of all my work, trying to teach her to spend her leisure properly.

JULIAN. It was a very nice day.

CHARLES. What's that got to do with it?

JULIAN. I was trying to be indulgent.

CHARLES. You're not paid for indulgence, are you?

JULIAN. No.

CHARLES. Then get on.

JULIAN (*sitting on the settee; reading*) "Twelve-fifty-five subject leaves park and enters a cinema in Oxford Street. It was showing the film *I was a Teenage Necrophile*."

CHARLES. Did you go in after her?

JULIAN. With reluctance.

CHARLES. And she sat by herself?

JULIAN. Throughout. It was a very tasteless film. But worse ones were to follow. I mean, on subsequent days.

CHARLES. And that was how she spent her day?

JULIAN. Yes.

CHARLES. After all I've taught her. (*He moves up* RC) How dare she? How dare she? (*Upset*) I beg your pardon. It's not an easy thing to set detectives on your wife. (*He moves to* L *of Julian*) It must seem rather bad form to you— or it would if—well . . .

JULIAN. If I wasn't one myself. It still does, Mr Sidley. I must admit I end up despising many of our clients.

CHARLES. Despising? (*He crosses to* L *of the desk*) That's rather rich coming from you, isn't it?

JULIAN. Oh, yes, I dare say. It's something of a reflex action. They despise me, after all.

CHARLES. What else do you expect?

JULIAN. Nothing. The client looks down on the whore who relieves him. It's a familiar pattern.

CHARLES. Charming image.

JULIAN. But not inappropriate.

CHARLES (*crossing to* RC) If you think like that, why do you do it?

JULIAN. Private reasons. Or to be exact, public reasons.

CHARLES. I don't understand.

JULIAN. It's not important. At the risk of being impertinent, Mr Sidley, why did you come to us? You really had nothing to go on.

CHARLES. You mean nothing concrete. No letters written in a hot impetuous hand. No guilty smiles or blushes. My dear man, we live in the twentieth century, which blushes for nothing. The blush has gone out, like the ball-card and the *billet-doux*. (*He moves behind the desk*) Betrayal has become a word with rather quaint connotations.

JULIAN. I think that's just rhetoric, Mr Sidley. Rather well managed, if I may say so, but not true at all.

CHARLES. No? My wife has no more conception of sexual fidelity than this chair. (*He moves to* L *of the desk*) When I married her, she thought nothing of sleeping with three different men in the same week.

JULIAN. Was one of them you?

CHARLES. I don't think I need to answer that.

JULIAN. Oh, come. If you're like a priest in *your* profession, I'm like a psycho-analyst in mine. You can't afford to withhold information. Unlike an analyst, I'm not considered a gentleman, so you can tell me everything. If this was true, why did you marry her?

CHARLES. Because—I was infatuated with her.

(*There is a pause.* CHARLES *almost visibly unbends a little*)

JULIAN. Continue please.

CHARLES. I don't see what possible bearing this could have on the situation.

JULIAN. You must let me be the judge of that. Where did you meet her?

CHARLES. In a place called the *Up-To-Date Club* in Brewer Street.

JULIAN. It doesn't seem the sort of place you would go to.

CHARLES. I was taken there by a journalist friend, and I must say it was very pleasant. It had a dining-room up-stairs with French cooking and a sort of cellar below where you could dance. (*He moves below the desk*) I wasn't very good at dancing—at least not at all that jungle warfare they call dancing—(*he moves to* R *of the desk*) but the food was excellent, and Belinda served it.

JULIAN. Belinda?

CHARLES. My wife. She didn't serve it very well, either; she was always forgetting one's order and having to come back for it—which I found more agreeable than otherwise. I caught myself going there rather often. Finally I asked her out to a theatre. She's never seen anything more complicated in her life than a horror film. She was abso-lutely obsessed by horror films.

JULIAN. She still is.

CHARLES. Yes. It was rather a strange wooing. Without my demanding it, of course, she surrendered her whole life to me, for re-making. In a way, I suppose it wasn't too surprising. She'd lived in Northampton for the first eigh-teen years—her father was in shoes—and his ambitions for her extended no further than a job at the library and marriage with a local boy. Very properly she ran away to London. She fancied she had artistic talents.

JULIAN. And had she?

CHARLES (*with a step towards Julian*) Impulses, not talents.

She's a very good audience; a good viewer and a good reader. She is an excellent receiver, which is much more rare than most people imagine. Of course, when I met her first, her head was full of ridiculous rubbish about freedom and rebellion. She'd been leading the most extraordinary life, sharing a flat with two artists, one of whom baked his canvases in an oven, while the other spat paint on to his direct from his mouth, thereby expressing contempt for society, I believe. It's not surprising really that she reacted to a little tactful reform with enthusiasm. (*He crosses below the desk to* LC) For my part, I taught her everything I could. I'm not an expert, Mr Cristoforou; I'm that old-fashioned, but I hope not too comical thing, a dilettante. I know what is good. I see no reason for false modesty; what is the point of living at all, if one cannot rely on one's intelligence to learn from one's experience? Of course, the notion of an accountant with what, in the days when Europe was the world, used to be called a Soul, probably strikes you as ludicrous. I'm afraid there's a great deal about this situation which is ludicrous. The moral, of course, is that men of forty shouldn't marry girls of eighteen. It should be a law of the Church, like consanguinity: only marry in your generation. And yet it began so well.

JULIAN. You were happy?

CHARLES. Deeply. She renewed my life. I had someone to share things with: show things to.

JULIAN. And she? Did she show things to you?

CHARLES (*wandering* RC) She didn't need to. She was young and that was enough. Youth needs only to show itself. It's like the sun in that respect. In company with many men of my age, I found I was slipping away into middle life, journeying as it were into a colder latitude. I didn't like it. I didn't like it at all.

JULIAN. So you went after the sun. Tried to bottle a ray or two.

CHARLES. Foolish, imbecile attempt. Within a year I had to recognize that I had married a child. (*He moves up* RC) Someone with no sense of her place at all.

JULIAN. Her place?

CHARLES (*turning on him*) Certainly. Her place. I know

that's not a fashionable word, but that doesn't mean it has no meaning. Belinda is the wife of a professional man in a highly organized city in the twentieth century. That is her place. It dictates that she must live by a certain code. As I have often explained to her, this would undoubtedly be different if she were wedded to a jazz trumpeter in New Orleans, which she seems to think she is, but there still would *be* a code. (*He moves down* RC) There is no such thing as a perfectly independent person.

JULIAN. Is that what she wants to be?

CHARLES (*crossing to* L; *irritably*) I don't know what she wants to be. She doesn't know herself. Things have got steadily worse. Three months ago I invited a very important client to dinner; the President of one of the largest Investment Companies in the city. My wife presided over my table dressed in scarlet pyjamas. When I remonstrated with her, she said she was sick of stuffy guests.

JULIAN. It's a fair point.

CHARLES (*moving* C; *exasperated*) It's not a fair point. It doesn't mean my friends are stuffy, Mr Cristoforou, simply because they do not come to dinner disguised as motor-cyclists. Because they happen to prefer Mozart to *Stay loose, Mother Goose*. No doubt they are helplessly out of touch with modern living. They only read, think, travel and exchange the fruits of doing so pleasurably with each other. Is there anything so utterly boring and ridiculous as the modern worship of youth?

JULIAN. Nothing, no. It's like sun worship. Debasing and superstitious.

CHARLES (*looking suspiciously at Julian*) No doubt this is very amusing to you.

JULIAN. How can you think that?

CHARLES. You think it's sour grapes?

JULIAN. Of course not.

CHARLES. Oh, yes. I see that.

JULIAN. Mr Sidley, I beg you . . .

CHARLES (*with real pain*) Has my wife a lover? (*He moves* RC)

JULIAN (*rising and moving to* R *of Charles*) What makes you think she has?

(*There is a pause*)

CHARLES (*in a defeated voice*) Because for three months now she has turned away from me. Just turned away. You know how women avert their faces when they don't want to be kissed. Well, she is averting her face, her look, her mind. Everything. Whole meals go by in silence, and when she talks, she appears not to be listening to what she herself is saying. In the old days she used to stay in bed until long after I'd gone to the office. I used to remonstrate with her about it. Now she's up and out of the house sometimes before eight—as if she can't bear to lie in my bed another minute. Last week one morning she was up at six. When I asked her where she was going, she said she wanted to watch the sun come up from Parliament Hill. (*Explosively*) God damn it, d'you think I'm a fool? She's seeing someone else, isn't she? Look—last night she didn't come in at all.

JULIAN. At all?

CHARLES. Well, not until well past two. And not one word of explanation.

JULIAN. Did you ask her for one?

CHARLES. If I ask her for anything, that's a quarrel in a minute. (*He pauses*) Tell me. There's someone else, isn't there?

JULIAN (*quietly*) Yes. (*He moves behind the settee*)

CHARLES. Go on. (*Preparing for the shock, he sits on the settee at the upstage end*)

JULIAN. I find this hard.

CHARLES. Go on. How often do they meet?

JULIAN. Every day.

CHARLES. Every day.

JULIAN (*moving up* R) Yes.

CHARLES. Describe him.

JULIAN. Well—he's handsome, I'd say.

CHARLES (*bitterly*) Of course.

JULIAN (*crossing above the settee to* RC) Full of a kind of confidence: you know—debonair, rather elegant. I'd say he was a diplomat.

CHARLES. A diplomat?

JULIAN. Yes.

CHARLES. A diplomat? (*He pauses*) There was that party at the Nicaraguan Embassy.

JULIAN (*moving to R of the desk*) No, he's definitely not Nicaraguan.

CHARLES. How do you know that?

JULIAN. Ah! That's a very fair point. You have an acute mind, Mr Sidley. I admit that when you meet a complete stranger for the first time there is no definite way of knowing he's not Nicaraguan.

CHARLES. How does he behave to her?

JULIAN. With great politeness. He shows a most striking restraint.

CHARLES. You mean they don't actually kiss in public?

JULIAN. Certainly not.

CHARLES. What *do* they do, then?

JULIAN. Oh—stare at each other happily. Exchange looks of deep meaning. Give those little secret smiles—you know—I think the French call them *oeillades*. I'm sure that's the word. Shall I look it up? (*He moves to the bookshelves L and looks at them*) Where's your French dictionary?

CHARLES. Secret smiles . . .

JULIAN (*turning and moving LC*) I'd say, watching from a distance, their relationship was one of the utmost tenderness.

CHARLES. Would you?

JULIAN. Yes, I would.

CHARLES. Damn her!

JULIAN (*moving below the desk*) Mr Sidley . . .

CHARLES. Damn her! Damn her! (*Furiously*) What's his name?

JULIAN. I don't know.

CHARLES. Where does he live?

JULIAN. I don't know.

CHARLES (*rising*) Liar!

JULIAN (*moving RC*) I don't.

CHARLES (*grabbing Julian and swinging him to R*) Listen to me. You're a private detective, aren't you?

JULIAN. You know I am.

CHARLES. And it's your job to find out names and addresses?

JULIAN. I suppose it is.

CHARLES (*shaking him*) Well, you find out this man's name and address by tonight or I'll break your bloody neck. (*He hurls Julian on to the settee*)

JULIAN. Mr Sidley! I'm a professional man. You've no right to handle me like that.

CHARLES (*standing over Julian*) You're a sneaking, prying, impertinent little rat.

JULIAN. I didn't want to tell you. You made me. Be honest. You made me.

(*The buzzer of the intercom sounds.* CHARLES *hesitates briefly, then goes to the desk and depresses the switch of the intercom*)

CHARLES (*into the intercom*) Yes? Who is it?
BELINDA (*through the intercom*) Surprise, surprise.

(CHARLES *releases the switch and turns to Julian*)

CHARLES (*amazed*) My wife! She hasn't been here in over a year. You'll have to slip out the back way. (*He takes out his keys, moves to the door up* RC *and unlocks it*)

JULIAN. Why?
CHARLES. Do as I say.
JULIAN. No.

(*The buzzer sounds.* CHARLES *goes to the intercom and presses the switch*)

CHARLES (*into the intercom*) Yes. (*He releases the switch*)
BELINDA (*through the intercom*) Charles?
CHARLES (*pressing the switch; into the intercom*) I'm coming. (*He releases the switch and turns to Julian*) Through there, down the fire escape, into the mews.

JULIAN. No.
CHARLES (*crossing to* L *and collecting Julian's brief-case*) Please, I'm sorry I pushed you, you're quite right, you're a professional man. (*He crosses to Julian*) I apologize. Only please go.

JULIAN. No.
CHARLES. Why not?
JULIAN. I haven't finished my report. There's lots more yet when I can untangle the pages.

CHARLES. Look, come back on Tuesday.
JULIAN. I told you I hate Tuesdays.
CHARLES. Well, Monday, then. Six o'clock.
JULIAN. Five.
CHARLES. Five-thirty.
JULIAN (*rising*) Done.

(JULIAN *takes his brief-case from* CHARLES *and exits to the inner office, closing the door behind him.* CHARLES, *seeing the empty Yoghurt carton on the desk, puts it in a desk drawer. The buzzer sounds.* CHARLES *presses the switch*)

CHARLES (*into the intercom*) Yes. (*He releases the switch*)
BELINDA (*through the intercom*) What's going on up there?
CHARLES (*pressing the switch; into the intercom*) Nothing, my dear. (*He releases the switch*)
BELINDA (*through the intercom*) Well, open the door, then. It's still locked.
CHARLES (*pressing the switch; into the intercom*) Oh! Yes—I'm sorry. (*He presses the door release button*)

(*A buzzer sounds off* R.
JULIAN *enters from the inner office*)

(*To Julian*) What is it now?
JULIAN. My macaroons!
CHARLES. Oh, for God's sake!
JULIAN (*collecting them from the desk*) I can't possibly go without them.
CHARLES. Get out!
JULIAN. They're flown in daily from Vienna.

(JULIAN *runs out through the inner office, closing the door.*
BELINDA SIDLEY *enters* LC. *She is a pretty young girl of twenty-two, wearing a coloured blouse, slacks and a black sombrero with a pink carnation tucked into the brim. She is screened by an enormous bunch of yellow chrysanthemums*)

BELINDA. Charles, behold! I bring you blooms from the exotic East. Aren't they marvellous? There was a man selling them at the corner. I think he was a Malayan. Anyway, he had topaz eyes. So I bought his whole barrow, three quid with the greenery. (*She crosses to the settee and puts the flowers on it*)

CHARLES (*coldly*) Why aren't you at the *Cordon Bleu?*

BELINDA. I got tired of learning the right way to hold a saucepan, so I left. (*She removes her hat and puts it on the downstage window-sill*)

CHARLES. And came here.

BELINDA. Obviously.

CHARLES. Why?

BELINDA. I was just passing.

CHARLES. Passing?

BELINDA. Well, I thought I'd come and collect you. Surprise, lovely surprise! The Malayan said if I bought everything there'd be no monsoon over my temple for a year. Wasn't that a sweet thing to say? (*She picks up the flowers*)

CHARLES. Fairly uninspired, I'd say. The gypsy who sold you one sprig of heather last week for five pounds did rather better. (*He crosses and stands up* R *of the desk*)

BELINDA. Oh, that was because he belonged to a dying race, and I couldn't bear it. (*She moves to the umbrella-stand, removes Charles' bowler, puts it on the upstage window-sill, then puts the flowers in the stand*)

CHARLES. Belinda! This is only my office.

BELINDA. I know where it is, Charles. And it needs them. (*She goes to her hat and takes the carnation from it*)

(CHARLES *watches bitterly*)

(*She moves to Charles*) Are you feeling well?

CHARLES. Perfectly.

BELINDA. You don't look it. (*She puts the carnation into his buttonhole*)

CHARLES. How do I look?

BELINDA. The way you are when your chilblains itch. Irritable and sorry for your little self.

CHARLES. Very humorous.

BELINDA. How awful it must be to belong to a dying race. Like the Yaghan Indians. (*She crosses below the desk to the library steps*) I read somewhere there were only nine Yaghans left, right at the bottom of the world. No, honest.

South Chile. After a while Nature says, "Scrap them" and they just fail, like crops. Imagine them. Nine little shrunk people, sitting on green water, waiting to die. (*She climbs the steps and sits on the top*)

CHARLES  I am imagining them.

BELINDA.  What's the matter with you? (*She takes a book from the shelves, and opens it to read*)

CHARLES (*crossing to Belinda*)  It's a pity I'm not a Yaghan Indian, isn't it? I might get a little attention from you. Yes. Outrageous demand for a husband to make of a wife, isn't it? Attention. (*He shuts the book*) Notice.

BELINDA.  I notice you, Charles.

CHARLES (*moving to L of the desk*)  Very humorous. Ha! Ha!

BELINDA.  It's not meant to be.

CHARLES.  Where were you last night?

BELINDA.  Out.

CHARLES.  You knew I was bringing someone back.

BELINDA.  You said you might.

CHARLES.  Well, I phoned you from here at six and you weren't home.

BELINDA.  Well, so? Did you need me to pour out whisky or cut his cigar?

CHARLES.  That's hardly the point.

BELINDA.  It's just the point, I'd say. You always say you want me to entertain your friends, and as soon as you can you get out the port and send me out of the room. It's incredible, anyway, that a man of your age should be pushing decanters of port clockwise round a dining-table. It makes you look a hundred. When I tell my friends, they can't believe it.

CHARLES.  I'm sure they can't. But then, one would hardly accept their notions of etiquette as final, would one?

BELINDA.  Oh, please!

CHARLES.  What?

BELINDA.  Not your iceberg voice. I can't bear it. "One would hardly say . . ." "I scarcely think . . ." "One might hazard, my dear . . ." All that morning suit language. It's only hiding.

CHARLES.  Indeed?

BELINDA. Yes, indeed. Indeed, indeed! People don't say "indeed" any more, Charles. It's got dry rot. (*She comes down the steps and crosses to* R, *balancing the book on her head*)

CHARLES. Where were you?

BELINDA. With my friends.

CHARLES (*moving* LC) Oh, of course. In some grotesque little coffee bar, I suppose.

BELINDA. Correct, as you would say.

CHARLES. Telling stories about me. The way I talk. The words I use. My behaviour at the dinner-table. Very loyal, I must say.

BELINDA. And where were you? In a Pall Mall Club, surrounded by a lot of coughing old men with weak bladders and filthy tempers, scared of women and all mauve with brandy? How lovely!

CHARLES. That's just disgusting.

BELINDA. You're telling me! (*She lies full length on the settee, with her head at the downstage end, and opens the book*)

CHARLES (*crossing to* RC) And where are you going now? I mean, where are you *passing* to to go to? Another coffee bar?

BELINDA. Perhaps.

CHARLES (*after a pause*) Belinda: what does "a wife" mean?

BELINDA. What?

CHARLES (*moving to* L *of Belinda*) Perhaps it's a word no-one has ever explained to you. Certainly they didn't in that squalid little registry office you insisted on going to, because you couldn't enter a church. Nevertheless, at the risk of appearing still more pompous, let me remind you, my dear, you made a contract with me. A contract of marriage. (*He takes the book from her, crosses to the library steps and replaces the book on its shelf*)

BELINDA (*sitting up*) Well, what about it? There's nothing in it that says a woman must drop her friends and take her husband's. I know it's always done, but I don't see it should be. I never promised to cherish all those mauve old men in sickness and in health. I love my friends: how can I be faithful to you if I'm unfaithful to them?

CHARLES (*coming from the steps*) May I ask what that means?

BELINDA. That you're not my only responsibility, that's what it means, and I'm not yours. You've got to be faithful to all sorts of people. You can't give everything to just one. Just one can't use everything. And you certainly can't *get* everything from just one. That's not reasonable to expect, is it? Just because you get sex from a man, it doesn't mean you're going to get jokes as well, or a someone who digs jazz. Oh, I know a husband claims the right to be all things to a woman, but he never is. The strain would be appalling.

CHARLES (*moving* LC) Charming.

BELINDA. It's true.

CHARLES. It's not true. You talk about people as if they were *hors d'oeuvres:* him for the herring, him for the mayonnaise, him for the pickled beetroot.

BELINDA (*rising and crossing to* R *of Charles*) But that's exactly it. How clever of you to think of a comparison like that. That's marvellous.

CHARLES (*gently*) Yes, well it's just stupid and immature. I suppose I really shouldn't expect anything else.

BELINDA (*moving above the desk*) Ta very much.

CHARLES. If you were a real woman, you wouldn't find it hard to receive everything from one man. To see everything in him, and hope to be everything in return. But it's beyond you, of course.

BELINDA (*moving up* R *of the desk*) Ta very much.

CHARLES. Oh, stop that.

BELINDA. Then *you* stop it. (*She moves to the umbrella-stand and handles the flowers*)

CHARLES (*moving behind the desk*) Listen to me, and try to understand. Stop fiddling with those flowers.

BELINDA (*moving behind the settee*) Well?

(*There is a slight pause.* CHARLES *collects himself*)

CHARLES (*moving to* R *of the desk*) Let me tell you something. Each man has all of those things inside him, sex, jokes, jazz and many more important things than that. He's got the whole of human history in him, only in capsule. But it takes someone who loves him to make those capsules grow. If they don't grow, he's not loved enough. And that kind of love can only be given by an adult.

BELINDA. Which I'm not. Ta very bloody much! Well, if I'm not, whose damn fault is it? This isn't my home. It's my school.

CHARLES (*moving to* L *of the settee*) That's not true.

BELINDA. Oh, but yes, it is, Charles. Just that. (*She pauses and looks seriously at him*) You *were* everything to me once. That was probably unhealthy, but it was true. I thought you were the most fantastic person I'd ever met. I never knew that one head could hold so much. On one afternoon—February the nineteenth, two years ago—you explained to me the Theory of Natural Selection, the meaning of Id, Ego and Super-Ego, and the structure of Bach's fugue in C sharp minor. Book One, Well-Tempered Clavier. I know because I wrote it all down in my diary. I adored it. I really did. You weren't showing off. These things came up naturally in your conversation. The world seemed so wide suddenly. You were the first person who showed me that that was the most important thing to be. Most of my friends are all feelings. They're just like moles bumping about in dark little burrows of feeling, never able to see anything in clear daylight—except their own nerves. And that was me, too. Feeling, feeling all the time—but never getting to understand anything. When you met me, I'd have said or done anything just to join in. I thought people would like me more if I liked what they liked. So I pretended all the time. In the end I couldn't tell the difference between what I liked and what I said I liked. Do you remember that day we played totem animals and I said yours was the llama? Well, mine was the chameleon. I made up my enthusiasm to suit my surroundings. (*Frankly*) You released me from all that. You gave me facts, ideas, reasons for things. You let me out of that hot black burrow of feeling. I loved you, then.

CHARLES (*dully*) Then.

BELINDA. Yes.

CHARLES (*moving behind the desk*) But no longer.

BELINDA (*after a little pause*) I don't know. Living with

you has taught me to respect my feelings—not alter them under pressure.

CHARLES. And I'm pressure?

BELINDA. You're always pressure.

CHARLES. But now it's bad?

BELINDA. Yes. Some of it. (*Earnestly*) Look, I know I was a pupil before. I admit it. And it was good. But you were different, then. (*She moves to* L *of the settee*) Now I feel you hate me half the time.

CHARLES (*sitting at the desk*) That's ridiculous.

BELINDA. Well, resent me, anyway. Like an awful headmaster. The beak. I feel I have to defend myself in front of you. I feel guilty.

CHARLES (*sarcastically*) Do you?

BELINDA. Yes. Guilty.

CHARLES (*picking up a black ebony ruler from the desk*) How surprising!

BELINDA. What d'you mean? You don't mean that . . . ?

CHARLES. Oh, how long are you going to pretend?

BELINDA (*moving* RC; *bewildered*) Pretend?

CHARLES. For someone who puts such a premium on her honesty, you make a pretty awful showing, don't you?

BELINDA (*faintly*) What?

CHARLES (*quietly*) I know, my dear. I know. So there's no need for any of this.

BELINDA. Know?

CHARLES. About him. Your man.

BELINDA (*amazed*) You can't! You can't!

(CHARLES *and* BELINDA *stare at one another*)

CHARLES (*brusquely*) All right. Who is he?

BELINDA. There we go again. All right, come on. You can't say, "All right, who is he?" like that. (*She moves to the desk and takes the ruler from him*) School's closed, Charles. I'm sick of that tone of voice. I didn't marry it, and I've no obligation to it.

CHARLES (*rising and moving to* L *of the desk*) This is just quibbling.

BELINDA. No, it isn't. What right have you got to talk to me like that, ever?

CHARLES. The right of a husband. Like wife, my dear, a state of law. (*He sits on the left end of the desk, facing* L)

BELINDA (*moving below the desk*) Like wife, a state of mind. Can't you see that? Like marriage. Marriage is a state of mind. It's touching someone and not being able to take your hand away. If someone shakes that hand off, then you're not married. We're not married. We haven't looked each other in the eye for three months. I'm back in the old burrow of feeling again and I can't think at all. (*She sits on the downstage edge of the desk, facing front*)

CHARLES. Well, I'm not in any burrow, if you are. You think when marriage gets a little routine, you can disown it, like a bad bet.

BELINDA. I haven't disowned it.

CHARLES. No? Then perhaps you'd care to explain what else you've been doing these past three weeks?

BELINDA. I can't. Not to you.

CHARLES. I dare say not.

BELINDA (*rising, putting the ruler on the desk, then crossing to* L *of Charles and facing him*) Charles, answer me something. Do you love me? I don't mean want me, for whatever reason. I mean love me. Be honest.

CHARLES (*in a low voice*) Very much.

BELINDA. Then why the hell don't I feel it? "I'm burning," says the fire. But my cold hands say: "No, you're not." Love with me's a great burst of joy that someone exists. Just that. And with that joy comes a great need to go and greet them. That's the word: *greet*. I used to greet you like that, inside me, anyway, forty times a day. Now it's once a month. And always when you're not looking. When you've got your hat on at an angle trying to look jaunty, which you can never manage, or something like that. (*She moves to the steps and leans against them*) It's all so dead now with us.

CHARLES. And he's made you come alive?

BELINDA (*urgently*) Yes. *Yes*. Exactly that. *Alive.*

CHARLES. Suppose you told me.

BELINDA. You wouldn't dig it.

CHARLES (*dryly*) Well, give me the spade and let me try.

(BELINDA *laughs then looks very seriously at Charles*)

BELINDA (*gravely*) All right. I will, I *will*. Just listen. Don't say anything. Just listen and make what sense of it you can. (*She crosses to* RC) I don't make any, so we start equal.

CHARLES. Go on.

BELINDA. You know I've been going out by myself for weeks.

CHARLES. I had noticed.

BELINDA (*moving behind the settee*) I was trying to think: that's all. Trying to pull myself out of the burrow on my own. I wander all over the place, it doesn't matter where. Then one day, about three weeks ago, a man sat down next to me in the bus, turned and looked straight into my eyes. He was an extraordinary man.

CHARLES. Handsome. Debonair. The look of a diplomat, no doubt.

BELINDA (*surprised*) No, not at all like that. He was a goofy-looking man in a white raincoat, eating macaroons out of a polythene bag.

(CHARLES *gives Belinda a startled look, rises, turns and faces her*)

He had the funniest expression I ever saw, sort of witty. As if he wanted to wink, but didn't know how. At first I thought he was trying to pick me up, but it wasn't that. It took me a few minutes to work it out. What I was seeing was Approval. Do you know, I'd forgotten what it was like to be looked at without criticism? I was so embarrassed I got up and left. He immediately got up, too, and followed me. I began to walk very fast down Bond Street, and he walked just as fast behind, until we were both almost running. It was really quite funny. In the end I dived into Achille the hairdressers and had quite an unnecessary shampoo. He was waiting for me when I came out, leaning against Asprey's window sucking an iced lolly. Since then we've been together every day. I don't expect you to believe what I'm going to tell you, but it's every word true. (*She crosses to the front of the desk*)

CHARLES (*grimly*) Go on, please.

BELINDA. You're getting upset, aren't you?

CHARLES. Never mind me. Just go on.

BELINDA. I don't want to upset you. I really don't.

CHARLES. On!

BELINDA (*sitting on the downstage edge of the desk*) All right. First let me tell you the oddest thing about this whole affair. I call it an affair because it is one. Do you know, for the whole three weeks since we first saw each other, we haven't exchanged a single word? When I say we meet every day, I don't mean we make a date. All that happens is that everywhere I go he's sure to follow. (*She pauses*)

(CHARLES *avoids her eye*)

Like Mary's little lamb. He's a pure genuis at following. You never see him till he decides to show himself. Then he just pops up—click! Like that. In a coffee bar or a cinema, or out from behind a statue in the park. Once I turned round and there he was in the ladies' powder room at Fortnums. I suppose at the start I ought to have been scared, but I never was. Isn't that odd? I'd no idea what he wanted, and it didn't seem to matter. Of course, I realized he must be the loneliest man in town, but then in a way I was the loneliest girl, so it was sort of fitting. Who was I to complain if he got his kicks following me around? After a bit—and this is the really kooky thing—I began to get mine by following him?

CHARLES. You what?

BELINDA. The day came when he took over. I'd stopped outside a cinema where there was a horror film, and looked back as usual, just to make sure he'd see me go in. And you know, he shook his head. He wasn't going to see that film. He was like you, you see: he didn't really like horror films. Mind you, he'd had a bit of a do with them: I'd made him sit through eleven that week. Instead he turned round, signed for me to follow and marched off to the *next* cinema. That was the first time I'd ever seen an Ingmar Bergman film. Charles, they're wonderful! This one has a poor old man driving all over Sweden in a motor car,

looking for the turning he took wrong, years before. It's
pathetic.

CHARLES. No doubt.

BELINDA. It is, really. At one point he sees himself in his
own coffin.

CHARLES. And this is all you've got to tell me?

BELINDA. Yes. Anyway, as far as what you're thinkings'
concerned. After that the whole thing became marvellous.
We never knew what each day would bring. Sometimes *I'd*
lead, sometimes he would. (*She rises and moves* RC) Last
week I marched into the National Gallery and stopped in
front of Bellini's Portrait of a Doge. He was terribly grate-
ful: you know he'd obviously never seen it. He paid me back
by leading me out to Syon House, which is hidden away
behind all sorts of slummy things in Isleworth and has a
huge hall of green marble, and eight statues in gold, life-
size. (*She moves to the desk*) I know everything about him
now: even what he likes to eat. They're all sweet things—
he must be a Turk or something. Actually he dresses a bit
Turky. And he knows everything about me. One day we
were in a shop and he laid out that hat for me to buy. And
it's the only one I don't look stupid in.

CHARLES (*sitting on the left end of the desk*) Thank you.

BELINDA. Oh, Charles, it's not a question of hats. I've
had the most intimate relationship of my life with someone
I've never spoken to. What does it mean? When I'm with
him I live.

(CHARLES *stares at Belinda, with a numb expression on his
face*)

And because there aren't any words, everything's easy and
possible. I share all the time. I share—I share. Actually,
to be honest, it's me who feels guilty. Most of the time.
This morning I felt so bad I had to leave that stupid cookery
class and come here. I wasn't just passing. I wanted to
talk to you. No, I didn't. I knew that would be no good.
I wanted to—I don't know. Give you something. Those
flowers. Blooms from the exotic East. (*She crosses to the
flowers and looks at them*) They look a bit withered, don't
they? I'll get them some water. (*She opens the door* RC, *steps*

*into the office, disappears, screams, and runs out down* RC) Charles!

(CHARLES *rises and looks at Belinda.*

JULIAN *enters* RC *after her. He stands smiling nervously at Belinda. There is a pause*)

CHARLES (*to Julian; as if to a complete stranger*) Who are you?

JULIAN (*moving* RC) Good morning. My name is Cristoforou.

CHARLES. The office is closed on Saturday mornings. (*He moves behind the desk*) If you'd care to make an appointment . . .

JULIAN (*sotto voce*) We've already done that.

CHARLES (*moving to* L *of Julian*) What did I tell you to do?

JULIAN. Go down the fire escape into the mews.

CHARLES. Well?

JULIAN. I did, but the mews was so blank and abandoned. There was more life up here.

BELINDA. You know each other?

JULIAN. Your husband and I are new acquaintances. I don't think it will blossom beyond that.

CHARLES. How long have you been in there?

JULIAN. All the time. It was very illuminating. I mean your being so intimate. If you'd been exchanging remarks of general interest I'd probably have gone.

CHARLES. You mean you listened?

JULIAN. Of course. Eavesdropping is the second thing one is trained in, Mr Sidley. First shadow your man with your eye, then with your ear. It's an indispensable ability.

BELINDA. Charles, it's him!

JULIAN. He knows it is.

CHARLES (*moving* L) Don't . . .

JULIAN. I must.

BELINDA. Don't what?

CHARLES. No, please.

JULIAN. It's inevitable.

CHARLES. I forbid you to speak.

JULIAN. You can't. (*To Belinda*) I think you should sit down.

BELINDA. Who are you? (*She sits on the settee, at the down-stage end*)

CHARLES (*to Julian*) I'm your employer. Leave this house at once.

BELINDA. Employer?

CHARLES. Do you hear?

BELINDA. *Employer?*

CHARLES. Please—I ask you as a friend.

JULIAN. You're not a friend.

BELINDA. *Who are you?* Tell me.

(*There is a pause*)

JULIAN (*matter of fact*) I am a private detective, Mrs Sidley. Hired by your husband to spy on you.

(BELINDA *stares at Julian in stunned amazement*)

BELINDA (*faintly*) No. (*She looks at Charles*)

CHARLES. It was the only thing I could think of. I was at my wits' end.

BELINDA. No. Oh, no.

CHARLES. I know it was awful. But what else could I do? Your behaviour was so odd. You must admit that. Any husband would have been suspicious.

BELINDA (*breaking out*) No! No! No! No! *No!*

CHARLES (*moving below the desk*) Belinda . . .

BELINDA. Go away! You're filthy! Filthy! I never want to see you again as long as I live. (*She turns away from him*)

(CHARLES *looks on impotently*)

JULIAN. Well, you heard her. Go away.

CHARLES (*turning on him with a snarl*) What did you say?

JULIAN. I said go. It's what she wants.

CHARLES. You bloody meddling little wog! I'll teach you to make a fool out of me. (*He moves behind the desk and picks up the ruler*) Interfere with people's lives . . . (*He bounds towards Julian*)

(JULIAN *snatches up the statuette from the upstage window-sill and threatens Charles with it*)

JULIAN (*in a new, authoritative tone*) One step more and I'll interfere with your brains—what few of them there are.

(CHARLES *glares indecisively*)

I mean it, Mr Sidley. Coshing is the third thing a detective is trained in.

(CHARLES, *breathing hard, warily lowers the ruler*)

That's better. Now listen to me. I have done nothing to you at all.

CHARLES. Nothing. That's rich. Only stolen my wife's affections, that's all.

JULIAN. Your wife's affections weren't stolen, Mr Sidley. They were going begging. (*He pauses*) If you want them back, you'd better learn how to get them. For a start, go and take a walk round the gardens.

CHARLES. Are you talking to me?

JULIAN. *Do as I say.*

(CHARLES *looks speechlessly from one to the other, then exits by the door* LC, *taking the ruler with him. There is a pause.* BELINDA *sits on the settee, sniffling, not looking at* JULIAN, *who studies her for a moment in silence. He then replaces the statuette on the window-sill and addresses Belinda from behind the settee*)

Well. Why are you upset? Because your husband insults you by hiring a private detective? How strange. If I were a young woman, I'd be flattered to think a man could care so much about my virtue. After all, he's not a fool. He knows what the cost is of calling on someone like me. Disgrace, which only you can forgive. He's put himself in your power.

(BELINDA *does not respond or look at him*)

(*He moves to* R *of the desk and puts his brief-case on the floor beside it*) You don't care, do you? What's the matter? I'm not really the Fairy-tale Prince—is that it? I'm not a magic being who pops up in a lady's solitude, crying "Old loves for new"? My dear girl, of course I'm not. I'm a man, that's all. And not a very successful one, either. D'you think I enjoy being exposed like this? I'd rather keep my magic—which after all is only professional training in how to shadow.

The prince doesn't enjoy being turned back into the frog. But at least a frog is an understandable animal, whereas neither of us knows much about princes. If you really had to choose between one of those simpering aristocrats who did nothing but give banquets, and a decent, well-conducted frog, His Highness wouldn't get a second look. I'm right, aren't I? (*He pauses*)

(BELINDA *does not respond*)

Very well. Then at least let me jump out of the pond and explain the kind of frog I am. Yes?

(BELINDA *does not respond*)

Good. (*He moves above the settee*) My name is Cristoforou. Essentially I am—how can I explain it? I am a middle man. My first twenty-seven years were spent always making a third where two were company. I suppose it began when my mother divorced my unfaithful dad and married a stipendiary magistrate. (*He moves* RC) He looked on me as a foreigner, you see, which of course I was. Instead of telling him to go to hell, I tried to make him like me. That's an awful weakness in me, I'm afraid: the desire to be liked by everyone. When I was older I started becoming attracted to other people's wives. (*He moves below the desk*) Women who were unattainable obsessed me. Usually out of guilt I'd work up a friendship with the husband, and take a painful pleasure in being a constant guest in their home. Masochism, you see: very un-Latin. I was always in the middle, getting nothing and being generally in the way. Finally I made myself so unhappy I had to stop and think. One day I asked myself this fateful question: "Would you like to know a beautiful, tender, unattached girl to whom you were everything in the world?" And the answer came back: "No!" . . . Revelation! At that moment I realized something shattering about myself. I wasn't made to bear the responsibility of a private life. Obviously nature never intended me to have one. I had been created to spend all my time in public. This thought simply delighted me. It seemed to account for everything—all the unhappiness I'd ever suffered. Alone, I didn't exist; I came alive only against a background of other people's affairs.

(BELINDA *turns and looks at him, fascinated*)

Once I realized this, of course, it was the easiest thing in the world to select a permanent career. A detective was the obvious solution. I immediately resigned from Private Life, and became a Public Eye. A dick. (*He moves to Belinda, takes the bag of macaroons from his pocket and offers it to her*) Have a macaroon: they ease the heart.

(BELINDA *shakes her head*)

You think you're in love with me, don't you? Well, you're not. You're just not. Anyone would have done as well.

BELINDA. Ta very much.

JULIAN. I didn't mean it like that.

BELINDA. Get out!

JULIAN. Belinda . . .

BELINDA (*furiously*) Look: you've got no rights here. So why don't you just dick off to your dick's office?

JULIAN. How can you talk like that to someone who's been as intimate with you as I have?

BELINDA. Intimate?

JULIAN. Do you deny it? Do you dispute that we have spent three weeks in the city as blissfully as two people ever spent them in its history? Do you? Well, does that give me no rights? (*Earnestly*) How dare you? There is no sin more unpardonable than denying you were pleased when pleasure touched you. You can die for that.

BELINDA. What the hell are you talking about?

JULIAN. You know what I'm talking about, Belinda. You and I have exchanged our most personal treasures. And that makes rights. I'm the man who showed you Syon House, the Pool of London, the Isle of Dogs at dusk.

BELINDA. Well, it's not enough, is it? So get out.

JULIAN. I'm the man you showed Bellini's Doge. And Parliament Hill at six in the morning.

BELINDA. Well, that was my mistake. Just get out.

JULIAN. Oh, Belinda!

BELINDA. I hate you.

JULIAN (*leaning to her over the upstage arm of the settee*)
Impossible. I'm not a hateable man. Look into my eye.
No—look.

(BELINDA *looks reluctantly at him*)

(*He stares hypnotically at her, a few inches from her face*) What do
you see? I will tell you. You see one of the Seven Wonders
of Nature. The completely Public Eye—which looks
entirely outwards. Look into it. Beside this eye the eagle
is blind. The puma needs spectacles. Without immodesty
I tell you—this eye possesses the most watchful iris, the
most attentive cornea, the most percipient retina in the
Northern Hemisphere. (*He suddenly withdraws it from her
scrutiny*) And for almost a month it has been focused ex-
clusively on you. Just you. It has seen more in you than
anyone you ever met, or ever will meet. Think of that.
(*He crosses to* LC) And, I may add, it belongs in the head of
a man of taste and refinement who has been made to sit
through more execrable horror films than anyone should
be called on to see in a lifetime of duty. How dared you
inflict on me *Werewolves From Mars* and *Bloodsuckers From
Venus* both on the same day? If that doesn't give me rights,
what the hell in the whole world could? (*He removes his
raincoat and puts it on the library steps*)

BELINDA. You're quite mad, aren't you?

JULIAN. It's not a word I can define. If I am, humour
me.

BELINDA (*rising and crossing to* R *of Julian*) What d'you
want?

JULIAN. The usual thing. To be liked.

BELINDA. What d'you expect me to do? Go down on my
knees and thank you for making a fool of me?

JULIAN. Is that what I've done?

BELINDA. You know it is.

JULIAN. I don't at all. I found you aimless in London. I
gave you direction. I found you smileless, and gave you
joy. Not eternal joy, or even joy for a week. But immediate,
particular, bright little minutes of joy—which is all we ever
get, or should expect. Give over self-pity. It doesn't become
you. (*He crosses to the upstage window*)

BELINDA. Ta very much.

JULIAN. And give over saying that, too. It's hideous.

BELINDA. I'll say what I bloody want.

(JULIAN *looks out of the upstage window, then unfastens and opens it*)

What's he doing?

JULIAN. Beheading the dahlias with his ruler.

BELINDA. That's his way of working off anger. It's why I have to buy all my flowers off barrows. He's always knocking the dahlias about. (*She starts to cry*)

JULIAN (*crossing quickly to her*) Oh, please, don't cry. I can't bear tears. They're so excluding. Please. Please. Let me dry your eyes. (*Seductively*) Belinda. A simple service from a simple friend. Eye-drying while you wait. *Voila!* (*He pulls out the yellow handkerchief which he stuffed into his pocket at the beginning of the play. Belinda is showered with nuts and raisins*) Oh, misery!

(BELINDA, *astounded, bursts into laughter*)

I'm agonized! Utterly agonized. Did I hurt you? (*He brushes her down*) I'm sure I did. Nothing can hurt more than a brazil nut aimed with force.

(BELINDA *laughs harder, and takes the handkerchief from him*)

And the carpet. Ohhh! Look at them—all over it. (*He falls to his knees on the carpet and starts picking up the raisins and popping them in his mouth as he talks*)

(BELINDA *kneels, too, and helps to pick up the raisins*)

And such a *gorgeous* rug. Real Bokhara. I can tell. I used to sell them once, door to door, wearing a fez and a terrible stick-on goatee beard. Some dreadful gimmick of my employers. I looked like an extra out of *Kismet*, and sold nothing at all, *ever*, not even a Welcome mat.

(BELINDA *stops laughing*)

(*He offers her a raisin from the floor*) Would you like one?

BELINDA. Your need's greater than mine.

JULIAN (*seriously*) Will you give me one more minute before you throw me out?

BELINDA. Well?

(JULIAN *squats cross-legged in front of her*)

JULIAN. Look: this is my last day as a private detective. After your husband gets through with me, I can't hope to go back to Mayhew and Figgis, or anybody else. It's just as well. I was on the point of resigning, anyway. You can't imagine how wretched the job is. How unworthy.

BELINDA. I thought you loved it.

JULIAN. I thought I would, too. But I reckoned without my awful desire to be liked. Well, if you're a detective you can't be. If you give your employer bad news he hates you. If you give him good he thinks his money's been wasted. Either way you can't win.

BELINDA. Well, I don't see how I can help.

JULIAN. Oh, but you can. On my last day, you alone can help me. You can get me back my self-respect.

BELINDA. Me?

JULIAN. Yes, Belinda. I've spent three years helping to break up people's marriages. Don't you think it might recompense them a little, if I helped to preserve yours? Let me be honest with you: I'd like to be the first detective to *cement* a marriage.

BELINDA. That's a lovely thought, but I'm not going to stay with Charles to oblige you.

JULIAN. Why not? You owe me something.

BELINDA. I do?

JULIAN (*rising*) Certainly. You made me betray a job, which I've never done in my whole life before. If anything, *I* should be furious with *you*. You're a *femme fatale*.

BELINDA (*grandly crossing and sitting on the settee*) Oh, I'm sure!

JULIAN (*crossing to her*) It's true. You destroy men's integrity.

BELINDA. You just said the job didn't have any.

JULIAN. Don't quibble. (*He kneels at her feet. Ardently*) I knew as soon as I ever saw you, standing all alone in the mists of Hyde Park, throwing acorns at the ducks. There was something about your loneliness that filled my eyes with tears. I tasted at a distance the salt of your solitude. After a week of following you about, staring aimlessly into windows, crumbling endless filthy cakes in endless loathesome coffee-bars, I did something which my whole training was powerless to prevent. I sat down beside you in a bus, and smiled. Your hand, Belinda. (*He takes her left arm and puts it around his neck*) Darkness shades me. On thy bosom let me rest. I quote as you may imagine.

BELINDA (*taking her arm away and giving him a push*) Look, there are limits to humouring the mad, and I've reached them.

JULIAN. You love your husband. You admitted it to him before. Or at least all your wish is to find your way to him.

BELINDA (*rising and crossing to* LC) Oh, stop!

JULIAN. What?

BELINDA. All that magaziny language.

JULIAN (*rising*) I've got a magaziny mind. (*He sits on the settee*) You've found me out. I should never have talked. When I was dumb we understood each other.

(BELINDA *moves behind the desk, kneels on the desk chair and leans across the desk*)

BELINDA. If there's any finding ways back to be done, it's by him—not me. If you'd known him as he was you'd have adored him. He used to be gay—really gay. He used to say hundreds of funny things and then laugh at them himself, which I think's a marvellous sign, to laugh at your own jokes. It means you're *in* life. Now, he's sort of out of it, sarcastic and gritty, as if something's drying him up.

JULIAN. It is.

BELINDA. What?

JULIAN. Jealousy.

BELINDA. Jealousy? If anyone should be jealous it's me. (*She sits in the desk chair*)

JULIAN. What d'you mean by that?

BELINDA. Nothing.

JULIAN. You mean he's unfaithful to you?

BELINDA. Oh, no, not really. He takes himself off to a pro sometimes, somewhere in Ladbroke Grove. That's not really unfaithful. He'd die of shame if he thought I knew.

JULIAN. How *do* you know?

BELINDA. A friend of mine saw him going in one day. Her name's Madame Rita, which is lovely for a pro, isn't it! I mean, you can just see her, sort of Bermondsey Brazilian. He must have found her in the Ladies Directory.

JULIAN. What on earth's that?

BELINDA. Don't you know—it's a sort of underground directory of pros. Costs a pound. Charles is riveted by it. He keeps a copy in his desk.

JULIAN. Oh, you poor thing.

BELINDA. Not at all. It served me right for prying.

JULIAN. And you're not jealous?

BELINDA. Of course not. I think it's very sensible of him. Men should often have a change from their wives. It makes for a happy home.

JULIAN. I haven't noticed it in your case.

BELINDA. Nor have I. What d'you mean—he's jealous? What's he jealous of?

JULIAN (*rising and crossing to* R *of her; gravely*) All your personal life which he hasn't given you. When you married, you were his pupil. He talked, you listened. Then one day, as you said, school closed. The chameleon began to change into a princess. (*He stands behind her*) Your own thoughts sprouted and you turned into yourself. That's what he can't forgive: your life outside of him. It's not really unusual. Many husbands want to create wives in their own image: they allow a certain growth—so far and no farther. (*He moves to* L *of her*) Thereafter they will resent all changes they haven't caused, all experiences they haven't shared, and—with wives brighter than they—all new things they can't keep up with.

BELINDA. But I'm not brighter than Charles.

JULIAN (*moving* LC) Oh, Belinda—a million times.

BELINDA (*astonished*) Me?

JULIAN. Of course. Do you want to know what I think about your Charles?

BELINDA. What?

JULIAN. I think he's pitiful.

BELINDA. He isn't.

JULIAN. He's so afraid of being touched by life, he hardly exists. He's so scared of looking foolish, he puts up words against it for barriers: Good Taste, Morality. What you *should* do, what you *should* feel. He's walled up in Should like in a tomb.

BELINDA. What a marvellous comparison.

JULIAN. It's true, isn't it?

BELINDA (*rising and moving to the upstage window*) I suppose it is. (*She looks out at Charles*) Poor Charles.

JULIAN. Lucky Charles, to have you. Because he's sick and you're well.

BELINDA. He's not sick. He's just a bit stuffy, that's all. (*She moves to the downstage window*)

JULIAN. Sick. If you hear a piece of music, you'll either love it or hate it. He won't know what to feel till he knows who it's by. Sick. You can say "nigger" and have black friends. He'll only say "negro"—but dislike them.

BELINDA (*moving behind the settee*) That's true.

JULIAN. Sick.

BELINDA. Go on. More.

JULIAN. You're Spirit, Belinda, and he's Letter. You've got passion where all he's got is pronouncement.

BELINDA. More! More!

JULIAN. There is no more. He's half dead, and only you can save him. The choice is yours: walk out, and he dies. Stay, and with all your efforts you might just bring him back to life.

BELINDA (*surprised*) You're not mad at all. You see everything.

JULIAN. Of course. I have a public eye.

BELINDA. But you scare me.

JULIAN. Why?

BELINDA. Because it's too much. I can't be that responsible. I mean it: it's too much.

JULIAN. It's a lot, yes.

BELINDA. And what can I do, after all?

JULIAN. That depends on what you want to do.

BELINDA. Why can't you ever answer a straight question with a straight answer?

JULIAN. All right—(*he crosses to* RC) a straight question first. Do you *want* to do anything for him? Be utterly honest.

BELINDA. You know I do.

JULIAN. Good, then teach him as you taught me. Don't you know what you did for me? You gave me a private life. For three weeks I walked through London, all alone except for you to point the way. And slowly, for the first time since I can remember, I began to feel my own feelings. In the depths of that long silence I began to hear the rustle of my own emotions growing—at first just one or two little shoots, quick to die—then thicker, stronger—my very own feelings, Belinda, my very own reactions. And I was no longer displaced. I was the being who contained this rustling. You talked about burrows of feeling without thought. But there's something worse: burrows of not feeling anything. Burrows of deadness. Numbness. Burrows of sleep and torpor where you hide away from experience because you are afraid of changing. Like him. Clinging to a past self that festers when it's clung to.

(BELINDA *crosses below the settee to Julian*)

(*He takes her hand*) You led me out of those burrows, Belinda. Now, lead him the same way. Eurydice leading Orpheus for a change.

BELINDA. Who were they?

JULIAN. Lovers who found their way back from Hades by not looking at each other. Only you do it by not speaking, which is so much better than this babel we're all in. How many people would stay married, in your fact as well as his law, if they just shut up, and looked, and listened, and heard each other's heartbeats in the daytime.

(*There is a pause. They look at one another*)

(*He kisses her hand*) You gave me the only gift I really needed. Now give it back to him.

BELINDA. How?

JULIAN. The same way. In silence.

BELINDA. You mean not talk to him?

JULIAN. Of course. It's his only chance.

BELINDA. But that's impossible.

JULIAN (*excited*) Of course. Of course. Of course. (*He crosses quickly to the upstage window, leans out and calls*) Mr Sidley! Come in here at once.

BELINDA (*moving to R of the desk*) What are you going to do?

JULIAN (*moving to her*) Do you trust me?

BELINDA. No.

JULIAN. You asked for a straight answer. Well, you're getting one. (*He crosses below the desk to LC*) Do you want to return to your marriage?

BELINDA (*moving down RC*) Yes, I do.

JULIAN. Then do exactly as I say. Do you promise?

BELINDA. I don't know why I should.

JULIAN. Put yourself completely under my orders for a month. I promise in return it'll work.

BELINDA. For a month?

JULIAN. Unavoidable. Promise.

BELINDA. A month's for ever.

JULIAN. It's four weeks. Promise.

BELINDA. I think you really are mad after all.

JULIAN. Promise.

BELINDA. Yes.

JULIAN. You break it and you'll go to hell. (*He goes to Belinda and places her by the upstage end of the settee*) Stand there. When he comes in, don't look at him. And whatever happens, don't speak. (*He crosses to LC*)

BELINDA. Don't speak?

JULIAN. Not a single word.

BELINDA. That's idiotic.

JULIAN. Are you questioning me?

BELINDA. Yes. (*She moves from her position*)

JULIAN. Oh, well, then the game's off. There's no fun playing Master and Slave if you're going to question everything.

BELINDA. No, I'm sorry. I'll behave. But keeping quiet's a bit brutal. (*She goes back to her position*)

JULIAN. Well, you'd better get used to it. You're going to have to do it for a month.

BELINDA. A month? (*She opens her mouth in surprise*)

JULIAN. Ssh! Here he comes. Stand up straight. Look proud and all that. (*He backs to L of the library steps*)

(BELINDA *stands like a statue up* RC, *facing front.*
CHARLES *storms in* LC. *He still has the ruler*)

CHARLES. Well? Who are you shouting at?

JULIAN. You.

CHARLES (*moving behind the desk*) Belinda, I think it's time
we went home, don't you?

(BELINDA *does not look at Charles, or respond at all*)

We can discuss it all later, at home.

JULIAN (*leaning on the steps*) There's nothing to discuss,
Mr Sidley.

CHARLES. Belinda, listen to me, dear . . .

JULIAN. It's no good, Mr Sidley.

CHARLES (*very angry*) Now look: you've done enough
damage already. Whatever I've got to say, I'll say to my
wife. Alone. Now get out.

JULIAN. But that's just it, Mr Sidley. You have nothing
to say to her, and she certainly has nothing to say to you.
As far as you are concerned, she has renounced speech. I
am empowered to speak for her.

CHARLES (*urgently*) Belinda.

JULIAN. It's useless to address her. She will not reply. So
you had better listen to me, hadn't you? I bear her exact
and peremptory ultimatum. She is so shattered by your
conduct—setting a low, sneaking, prying wog of a detective
on her—that she is leaving you for ever.

CHARLES. Belinda! (*He puts the ruler on the desk*)

JULIAN. Unless . . . Yes, you are lucky. There's an Unless. You have one chance of keeping her. But only one.
That is—you will take my place in the streets of London.
(*Formally*) You will follow her every day for a month, at
a distance of fifty feet, wherever she chooses to go. You will
look at whatever she chooses to point at. You will hear
whatever she chooses to listen to. You will sit, stand, skip,
slide or shuffle, entirely at her will. And for all this month,
neither in study nor street, at table nor in bed, will you
exchange a single word with her. (*More easily*) If there's
anything special you want to see, and show her, then you
may lead. But it had better be good. This is your will, isn't
it, Belinda?

(BELINDA *nods*)

Inexorable, aren't you, Belinda?

(BELINDA *nods*)

The alternative is divorce.

(BELINDA *nods*)

Sunderment.

(BELINDA *nods*)

Endless separation.

CHARLES. Are you done?

JULIAN. Oh, yes. End of words, start of action. (*To Belinda*) Go forth, my fair Eurydice, go forth. Begin the long ascent into the day.

(BELINDA *and* JULIAN *look at each other very fondly.* BELINDA *collects her hat from the window-sill and slowly crosses to Julian.* CHARLES *follows Belinda down, then goes behind the settee*)

CHARLES. Belinda. Now, Belinda, listen. You're upset. You're distressed, and very reasonably. I concede this. But at the moment you're not thinking properly. You're regressing. (*He moves* RC) You're back in that burrow of feeling, that's all. I'm right, aren't I? You know I'm always right about you in the long run.

(BELINDA *hands Julian his handkerchief*)

JULIAN (*holding Belinda's hand a moment*) I suggest the *Hanging Gardens* for a start. Make him eat a Babylon Special.

CHARLES. Belinda?

JULIAN. No, make him eat two.

(BELINDA *exits* LC)

CHARLES (*crossing to the door* LC) This seems a good joke to you, but what are you really doing? You're acting on impulse, that's all.

(CHARLES *exits* LC)

(*Off*) You're living on pure emotion without thought or . . .
Belinda! *Belinda!* (*Faintly*) Belinda.

(CHARLES *re-enters, closes the door, then sits at the desk*)

If she thinks I'm going after her, she's mad.

JULIAN. I strongly advise you to follow her, Mr Sidley.

CHARLES. Do you? Do you indeed? Well, fortunately
you don't know my wife as well as you think. She'll get
tired of this nonsense in an hour. Now get out. And I may
as well tell you I'm going to see to it immediately that you
are fired. (*He rises, stands* L *of the desk and lifts the telephone
receiver*)

JULIAN. I'm agonized. Actually I have a much better job
to go to.

CHARLES. Indeed?

JULIAN. Yes. Yours. (*He crosses behind Charles and sits at
the desk*) I've made a decision. While you are outside doing
my job, I'll sit here and do yours. Exchange is no robbery,
as they say. And even if it is, robbery can be rather stimu-
lating.

CHARLES. Very humorous. (*He replaces the receiver*)

JULIAN. It may well be. I've always had a hankering
after the accountant's life. (*Into the intercom*) "Good morning, Miss Brown: bring me the Sidley Trust file, please."
"My dear sir, you have made a great deal of money. You
must look to pay a great deal of tax. However, there are
one or two—what can one say—loopholes, I believe, is the
vulgar word. I prefer 'modes of avoidance'."

CHARLES (*moving* LC) If you are not out of this office in
one minute by my watch, I shall call the police. I understand they are none too fond of your kind of person.

JULIAN. If you are not out of this office in thirty seconds
by my watch——

CHARLES. Well?

JULIAN. —I shall tell your wife about Ladbroke Grove.

(*There is a pause of surprise*)

CHARLES What d'you mean?

JULIAN. I'm not a private detective for nothing, Mr
Sidley. And I did give you warning I was a good one.

Once I was sure of your wife's innocence, I took to wondering about yours. So I followed you.

CHARLES. I don't believe it.

JULIAN (*lightly*) Madame Rita? Not exactly my type. We wogs prefer something more Home Counties. (*He rises and crosses to the bookcase* L)

(CHARLES *moves to* R *of the desk*)

Let's see. There ought to be reference books on the subject. I'm sure your superb collection must contain at least one encyclopaedia on matters sexual. One Almanac of Arcana? At the very least, a directory.

Charles (*his voice faltering*) Directory?

JULIAN (*crossing* RC *to the door of the inner office*) Perhaps it's in the Pornographic Section.

(CHARLES *puts himself between Julian and the door, barring the way*)

Ah: closed to the General Public!

CHARLES. How dare you?

JULIAN. Go through your desk? Routine procedure. You now have fifteen seconds, Mr Sidley. (*He sits at the desk. As he speaks, he picks up his brief-case from the floor, takes out a knife, a sugar canister and a grapefruit. He cuts the grapefruit in half, puts one half in a glass ashtray and takes another teaspoon from the desk drawer*) Look: as I told you, I never fail jobs, they always fail me. I can hold the fort here perfectly well for a month. I'll just sit here, turn all comers into companies, and let them enjoy themselves. After all, to be an accountant nowadays, you simply need a highly developed sense of fantasy. And I'm sure you'll admit I've got that.

(*The telephone rings*)

(*He lifts the receiver. Into the telephone*) Hallo? . . . No, this is Mr Sidley's assistant . . .

(CHARLES *makes a grab for the telephone*)

(*He rises, evades Charles and moves to* L *of the desk*) He's on holiday for a month . . . That's right: one month . . .

(CHARLES *makes another effort to grab the telephone*)

One moment, please. (*He quickly slips the receiver in the desk drawer, closes it, then looks very seriously at Charles*) Look, my dear man: don't be entirely stupid. Your wife's failing love may not be a deductible expense—but it's the only thing you've got.

(*There is a pause.* CHARLES *returns* JULIAN'S *stare, tacitly admitting the truth of this, then lowers his eyes and moves* RC)

(*He moves* LC. *As if to a child*) Go on. Or you'll lose her. (*He collects his raincoat from the library steps and crosses to Charles*) And put this on. It may help. Conditioned reflex, you know. (*He helps Charles on with the raincoat, collects the umbrella and the bowler hat, hooks the umbrella on to Charles' arm and puts the bowler on his head*) Remember, one month. I do know your wife, Mr Sidley, and I know she'll keep at it. But if by any small chance she wavers, you must insist. If you don't—Ladbroke Grove. Go on now.

(CHARLES *retreats to the door* LC)

(*He watches, smiling amiably*) I'll have the bill sent here, of course. It's more discreet, isn't it?

CHARLES (*turning in the doorway; viciously*) One thing, Mr Cristoforou. If I may remind you, you said that the man my wife met every day was handsome. Elegant, Mr Cristoforou. Debonair.

JULIAN. So I did, Mr Sidley. So I did. I thought it more tactful. I mean any husband can be excused for losing out to a dream figure like that. But to someone like me . . . ? (*He takes the receiver from the drawer. Into the telephone*) I'm sorry to have kept you waiting . . . Yes, he felt the need for a complete rest . . . Yes, he had to . . . go.

(CHARLES *exits* LC)

(*He sits at the desk*) Well, permit me to introduce myself. My name is Cristoforou. Julian Cristoforou. Diplomas in accountancy from the Universities of Beirut and Damascus. Author of the well-known handbook *Teach Yourself Tax Evasion.* What seems to be your particular problem? . . .

Fifteen thousand pounds Schedule A. Seventeen thousand
pounds Schedule D. It's monstrous! You haven't paid it,
I hope?. . . I'm delighted to hear it . . . Of course not. Paying any tax that is over five per cent of your total income I
consider a desperate imprudence . . . Yes, of course, we
have limitless experience in this field. Cristoforou and
Sidley. A firm of the very highest . . . (*He takes a spoonful
of grapefruit and pulls a face at its bitter taste. He picks up the
sugar canister and sprinkles the fruit, but it is empty. He bangs it
to shake the sugar loose, but to no avail*) I think you'd better
come round and see me immediately . . . No, my dear sir,
I assure you, we won't let the Government touch a penny
piece of your money. Not without a battle that would make
Fifteen thousand pounds Schedule D. Seventeen thousand
pounds Schedule B. It's monstrous! You haven't paid it,
come round in, shall we say, one hour? . . . Excellent. I
look forward to it. In the meantime, don't worry about a
thing. And if you could bring round with you a pound of
granulated sugar, I'd be greatly obliged. Good day to you,
sir . . . Good day!

*He replaces the receiver as—*

the CURTAIN *falls*

# FURNITURE AND PROPERTY PLOT

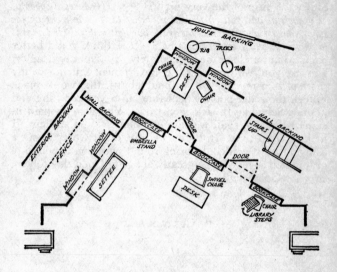

*On stage:*   *On window-sills:* pair Chinese statuettes

        Settee. *On it:* squab

        Large Cloisonne vase. *In it:* Charles' umbrella with bowler hat on handle

        Desk. *On it:* intercom, connected to microphone off **L** (practical); bell-push with lead connected to buzzer off **R** (practical); appointments diary, black ebony ruler, large glass ashtray (used for grapefruit); telephone

            *Front of desk (left end):* drawer (to receive telephone receiver); *(right end)* drawer with papers (to receive Yoghurt carton and spoon)

            *Back of desk (right end):* drawer with two teaspoons

Swivel chair
Mahogany chair
Library steps
3 rugs
*In bookshelves* L: practical shelf with two books
Light switches L of door LC
*In inner office:* kneehole desk. *On it:* telephone, blotting
        pad, large black cigarette box, brass table-lamp
        with shade, tray with papers
    *On window-sill:* 4 ledgers
    2 chairs
    Rug

*Set:* *On floor* C: Julian's brief-case (large week-end type) *In it:*
    polythene bag with small macaroons, 1 grapefruit, 1
    empty sugar canister, 1 carton of Yoghurt (part to be
    eaten) 1 greasy folder (foolscap) with 6 foolscap sheets
    stuck together, 1 sharp knife
Doors closed
Windows closed, but unlatched
*Off stage:* Bunch of yellow chrysanthemums in tissue paper

*Personal:* JULIAN: wrist watch, box of raisins and nuts, large
                yellow silk handkerchief, visiting card
        CHARLES: bunch of keys, spectacles
        BELINDA: black trilby with carnation in band

Any character costumes or wigs needed in the performance of
this play can be hired from CHARLES H. Fox Ltd, 25 Shelton
Street, London WC2H 9HX

# LIGHTING PLOT

**Property** fittings required: brass table-lamp with shade (non-practical)

Interior. An office. The same scene throughout

THE APPARENT SOURCES OF LIGHT are 2 windows R

THE MAIN ACTING AREAS are R, RC, LC and at a desk C

*To open:* Effect of bright sunshine

*No cues*


# EFFECTS PLOT

EQUIPMENT:   C *stage in floats:* Buzzer (intercom)
            Telephone bell
            *Off* R: Buzzer (practical from push on desk)
            *Off* L: microphone connected to speaker in intercom
            on desk

| | | |
|---|---|---|
| *Cue* 1 | JULIAN: "You made me." <br> *Buzzer sounds* | (Page 19) |
| *Cue* 2 | JULIAN: "No." <br> *Buzzer sounds* | (Page 19) |
| *Cue* 3 | JULIAN exits <br> *Buzzer sounds* | (Page 20) |
| *Cue* 4 | CHARLES presses buzzer switch <br> *Buzzer sounds off* R | (Page 20) |
| *Cue* 5 | JULIAN: ". . . I've got that." <br> *Telephone rings* | (Page 47) |